0 0001 6090858 8

SOUTHEAST

D1060654

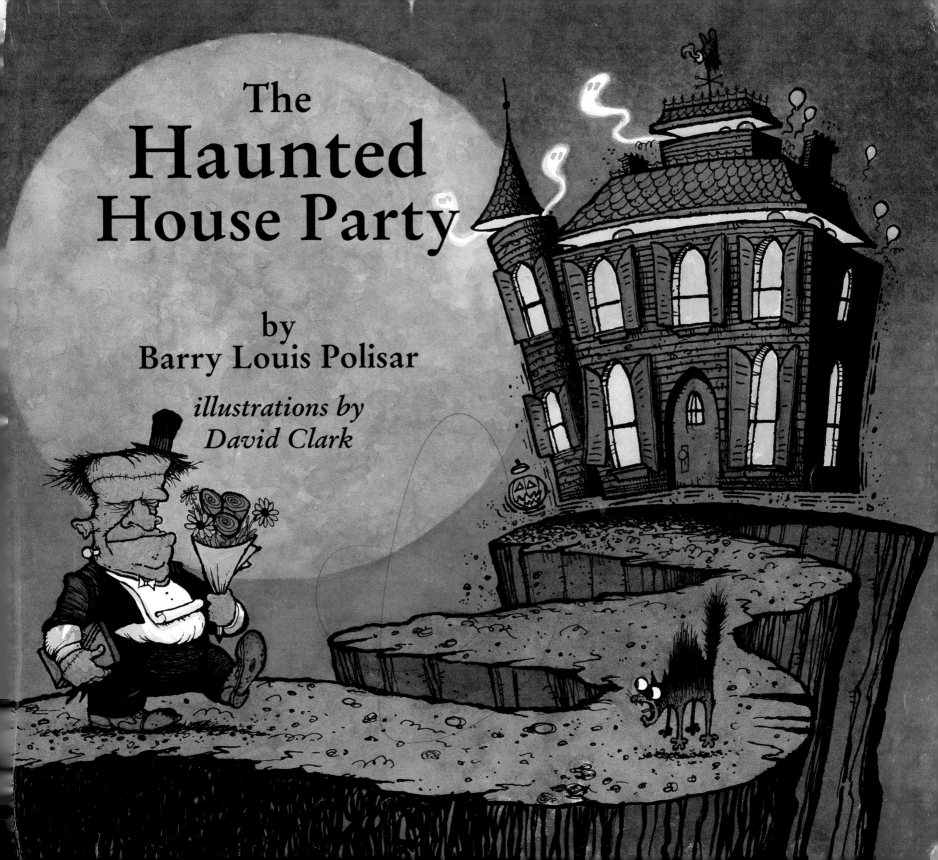

# The Haunted House Party

by
**Barry Louis Polisar**

*illustrations by*
*David Clark*

It was the night of Halloween.
    I thought I heard a shriek
And then a noise upon the stairs.
    I heard the floorboards creak
As if a ghost were in the house
    and coming very near.
I feared a weird and scary,
    hairy creature would appear.

My mom and dad had both gone out,
    nobody else was home
And I'd spent half the afternoon
    just talking on the phone
Inviting friends and making plans.
    I knew they'd soon be here.
I was alone—or maybe not—
    my heart was full of fear.

I heard a noise, the doorway shook.
  I hardly breathed at all
And then an Ogre entered
  at a parting in the wall.
He stamped his feet, he paced the floor,
  his finger poked the air.
Repeatedly he said to me,
  "Beware, young man, beware!"

"I know it's Halloween," he said,
  "and I've heard talk tonight
That you will have a party.
  Those you did not invite
Will bring you trouble—you will see.
  I've warned you to beware."
He spun three times and disappeared,
  left no trace anywhere.

Just like that! What did he mean?
    Oh, what was I to do?
My party was about to start
    and all my guests were due!
Who did he mean? How would I know?
    Each one would wear a mask.
How could I tell just who was who?
    I'd be afraid to ask.

Then suddenly I heard a knock
    and a howling, wailing sound;
The clattering beat of scattering feet
    running all around.
I heard a rattle, then a clack—
    was this some sort of joke?
A dozen skeletons came in.
    They rattled as they spoke.

Their bones all clacked like castanets
        and then, to my dismay,
They talked about my party
        and asked if they could stay.
I barely had a chance to speak
        when just beyond my reach
I saw an eerie spirit wave
        a ghostly hand and screech.

The doorbell started ringing.
        In came all sorts of ghouls
Mixed in with kids I recognized—
        and friends I knew from school.
But not all looked familiar.
        Some didn't use the door.
There were a few who I was sure
        I'd never seen before.

A bunch of friends came in a group,
    dressed as a Greyhound bus.
Denise came all dressed up in green,
    said, "I'm asparagus."
Mindy wore a cardboard box
    with a hole cut for her head.
Said, "I'm a condominium."
     "I'm Jello," Janice said.

I gazed upon the Ogre—
    his eyes were big and red.
My friends all gathered round him—
    "Great costume!," Marsha said.
I gasped for just a second.
    I knew she did not know
That he was not a party guest—
    I wanted him to go.

The lights went out. I heard a shout,
    then something grabbed my arm.
I screamed and heard a voice reply,
    "There's no need for alarm.
It's only me," Rebecca said
    as she took off her disguise.
"I didn't mean to scare you so. . . .
    Let me apologize."

"I'd like to play a game," she said,
    "It's really lots of fun.
Everybody gather 'round;
    I'll tell you how it's done.
Because it's Halloween we all
    should act the way we're dressed
And afterwards, we'll take a vote
    on which of us was best."

I interrupted her to say,
        "I think we should play darts.
Let's bob for apples or play chess—
        gin rummy, poker, hearts!!!
Any game but this," I said.
        "Let's play a different one."
But I was late in speaking . . .
        they'd already begun.

A ghost rose up under her sheet
        and danced around the place;
A baby ghost flew after her
        dressed in a pillowcase.
Although they danced politely,
        their friends were very rude—
In fact, two ghosts took off their sheets
        and flew completely nude.

The skeletons began to dance.
    The plates began to slide
Down from the shelf. They crashed and broke.
    I sat right down and cried.
My friends all stood around in shock;
    they dropped their masks and stared
With eyes the size of pumpkins,
    for they were very scared.

A little man with pointed horns
    was dressed up all in red;
He flicked his wrist, said, "Here's a trick,"
    and flames flew 'round his head.
The fire burned around him—
    he controlled it with his hand.
The flames licked at the ceiling
    and danced at his command.

A grisly witch then shouted out,
    "You want to see some tricks?
Watch this," she said and as she spoke,
    my mother's candlesticks
Flew through the air, then up the stair,
    and back down through the door.
"Show-off," the Ogre muttered,
    "I've seen that trick before."

The TV set did pirouettes,
    flipped on and off again.
Cups and plates danced figure eights—
    these guys were genuine.
Doorknobs spoke, lightbulbs smoked,
    the house began to move.
A goblin laughed and clapped his hands
    but I did not approve.

A noise came from the upstairs hall;
    I heard the bookshelves fall.
A ghost was reading poetry
    to entertain us all.
They say good poetry can serve
    to lift your spirits so—
But I'd had enough of spirits;
    I wanted them to go.

The doors dropped from their hinges.
    The shutters creaked and fell.
A sneaker burned inside my room;
    it made an awful smell.
The sofa had been ripped apart.
    The drapes were all in shreds.
Would Dad believe what happened
    when he saw my splintered bed?

Wires sparked, hot dogs barked,
  pumpkins blinked their eyes.
Potato chips dove into dips . . .
  emerged as butterflies.
The Ogre and the skeletons
  were dancing 'round the room.
Bones fell from the closet.
  The witch rode on our broom.

The house was swaying back and forth,
  each window pane was shattered
While ghosts and goblins carried on
  as if it didn't matter.
I stamped my foot and shouted out
  as I saw the curtains drop:
"This is my house and party,
  these are my friends—now *stop!!!*"

A pair of drunken skeletons
    passed through the closet door.
I scolded them and told them all
    that I could take no more.
"There's no excuse for what you've done;
    it's time to stop this stuff.
You've wrecked my house and party—
    and haunted me enough."

Trash was scattered everywhere.
    The wind blew through the door.
The house looked very different
    from the way it had before.
I knew that any minute now
    my parents would appear.
There was no way I could explain
    just what had happened here.

Then Michael grabbed the witch's broom
    and quickly swept the floor.
He said, "I'll help you clean this mess.
    They won't make any more."
The witch, embarrassed, then spoke up,
    said, "Listen quick to me—
With all these hands we'll make this house
    the way it used to be."

She waved her hand and with a flash
    the pots and pans returned
Back to the shelves from where they fell.
    She said, "Don't be concerned."
My bed was fixed, the books put back,
    the dishes all were done.
The drapes were quickly mended
    by a busy skeleton.

A goblin hung the shutters up
	and straightened out the shelves.
A ghost baked ginger cookies,
	and told us, "Help yourselves."
The plants and lamps were all returned,
	each to its proper place
As every sign of damage
	and destruction was erased.

The last guests left at midnight
	and as they drove away,
I heard a car pull in the drive
	and heard my father say,
"Hello . . . we're home . . . How did it go?
	Looks like you managed fine."
"I'm tired," I said, yawning . . .
	"What an exciting time."

We talked a bit, then said goodnight
    and I went up to bed.
I heard my mother talking.
    "He's growing up," she said.
"The whole house is so neat and clean,"
    Dad said in disbelief.
And I could sense, within his voice,
    a feeling of relief.

Mom started up the stairway
    when my father called her down.
I listened very carefully,
    but did not make a sound.
I heard my father talking
    as I rested, satisfied.
"Are those our candlesticks?"
    he asked, "How did they get outside?"

*This book is spine-tinglingly dedicated to*
*Roni Lynn Polisar*
*who has been Mrs. Polisar ever since*
*October 31st, 1981*

Once again, there have been many people who have helped with the production of this book. A very special thanks goes to Sheldon Biber who edited this manuscript and gave suggestions, ideas and support. Sheldon will always be my favorite ghost writer.

Thanks are also due Nancy Heller, who will always be a special spirit for her help in putting all the pieces together and helping me round out all the rough spots.

The Haunted House Party
by Barry Louis Polisar
© copyright 1981, 1985, 1987, 1995 by Barry Louis Polisar
Artwork © 1995 by David Clark

Published by Rainbow Morning Music
2121 Fairland Road, Silver Spring, MD 20904

First Edition
Hardback isbn #0-938663-21-6

A different edition of this book was previously published in 1987.